# for

**HUNTER**
the light of my life

**LYNN**
our gracious host

**ALESSA, ANDRÉS, CAMILA, DAISY, FIONA, JAYDEN, ELI, LEO, ROMÁN
BABY SANTOS, BABY TAUSCHER, ALL OF THE AXOLOTLS OF THE WORLD**
in the darkness is where you will shine the brightest

**MAMÁ**
por siempre recordarme como mantener mi brillo

**FRANZ**
for creating this beautiful story of light, letting me
embark on this journey for the first
time and for trusting me

Once upon a time, in a magical lake called *Xochimilco*...
(so-chee-meel-koh)

...a baby salamander was born.

But this was no ordinary amphibian.
This was a special type of salamander called an
**axolotl** and his name was **Tian.**
(ack-suh-lot-uhl)                    (tee-ahn)

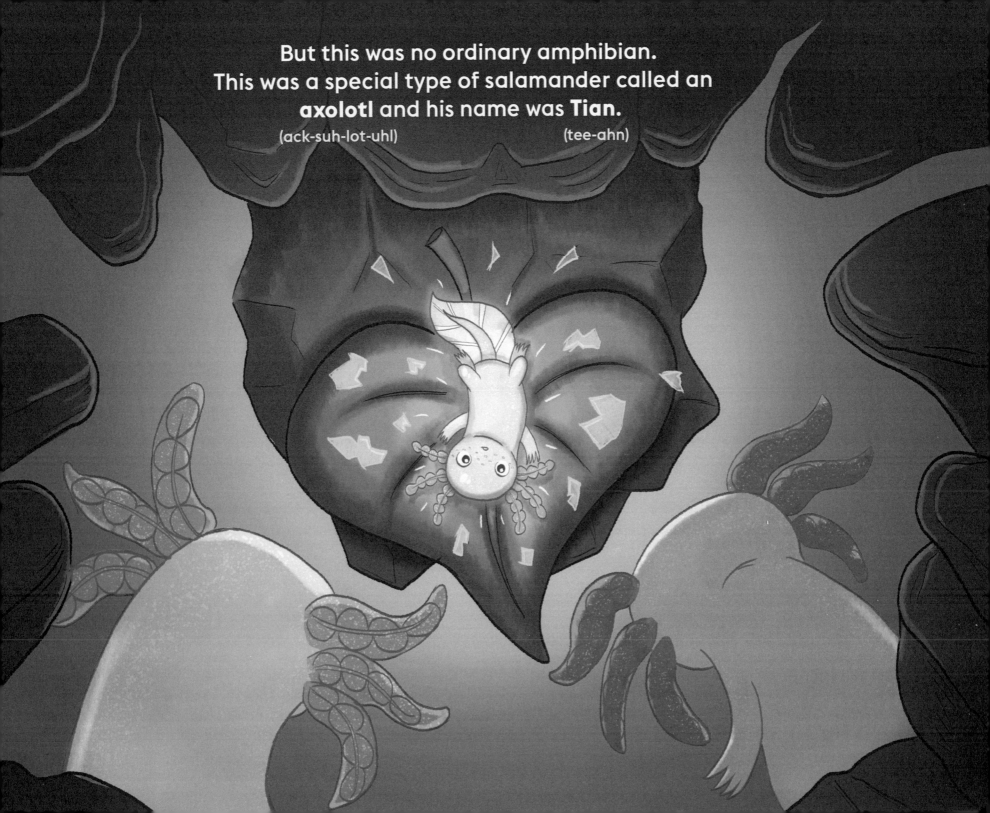

"Tian, my baby boy,
 you are too young to
 know this now but...

one day you will realize that
you were born to stand out.

You were born
to shine."

And as Tian got older
he noticed that he **DID** shine!

Unlike the other green and brown
salamanders around the lake,
Tian's skin gave off a
**bright, pink glow.**

And instead of lungs, Tian was born with gills.
On top of his head sat **six**, identical purple stalks.

Although Tian didn't understand why he glowed and nobody else did, the others were quick to make fun of his unique appearance.

All the taunting and name calling started to take its toll on Tian's confidence.

"Mom, do you think I'm ugly? At school they say only freaks have gills on their heads."

"Of course you're not ugly, son. Sometimes others make fun of things they don't understand, but that doesn't make you ugly. I think our gills are **beautiful**. They give us **life**. Without them we wouldn't be able to breathe underwater."

A few days later, Tian's curiosity struck again while they were out hunting for food.

"Mom, why is our skin color different from everybody else's?"

"Well, honey, our skin is lighter than others because that's just how we were made. One can't choose what skin color they're born with."

A week later, Tian's head was still full of questions.

"Mom, why aren't there more axolotls
like us in the lake?"

"Actually, baby, there are but since we are an endangered species...

...there are very few of us left. That's why it's important to stay away from the surface of the lake where all the big fish and humans are. It's not safe for us up there."

Tian spent the rest of that year doing what
a young salamander would do:

swimming with the fish...

...exploring the lake floor...

...and finding delicious food.

But when it came to fitting in, Tian simply **did not**.

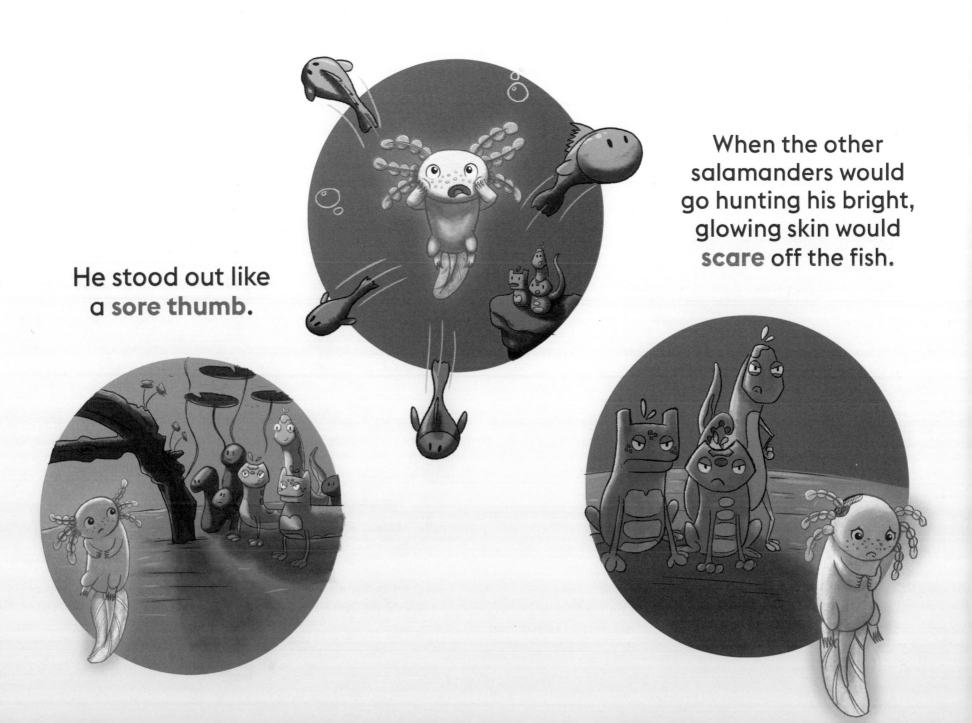

When the other salamanders would go hunting his bright, glowing skin would **scare** off the fish.

He stood out like a **sore thumb**.

And when they
would play
hide and seek...

Tian was always too
easy to find.

Eventually the other salamanders stopped inviting Tian to play. It seemed like the harder he tried to fit in the worse he felt about himself.

His bright, pink glow had even faded away.

... take this lake for example: its ecosystem depends on **all types** of creatures and plant life in order to flourish. Not everyone will accept or like the way you look, but you cannot let them change how you see yourself ...

... when you love yourself for who you truly are, you will glow brighter than all the stars in the sky."

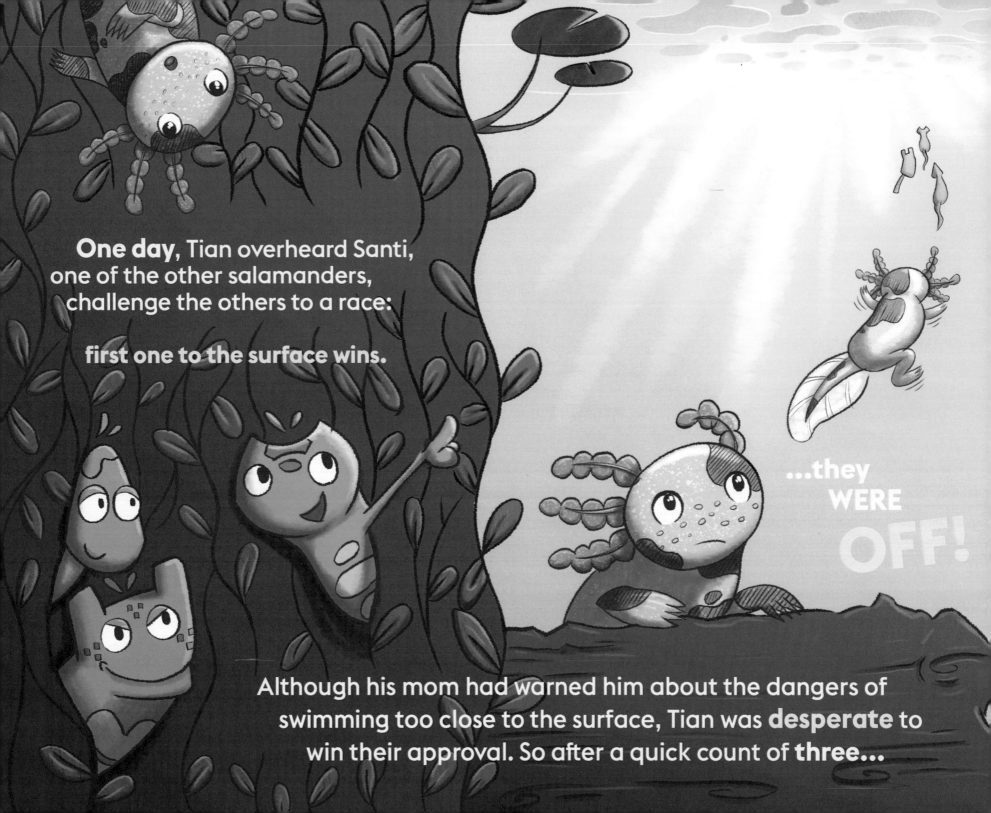

**One day**, Tian overheard Santi, one of the other salamanders, challenge the others to a race:

**first one to the surface wins.**

...they WERE OFF!

Although his mom had warned him about the dangers of swimming too close to the surface, Tian was **desperate** to win their approval. So after a quick count of **three...**

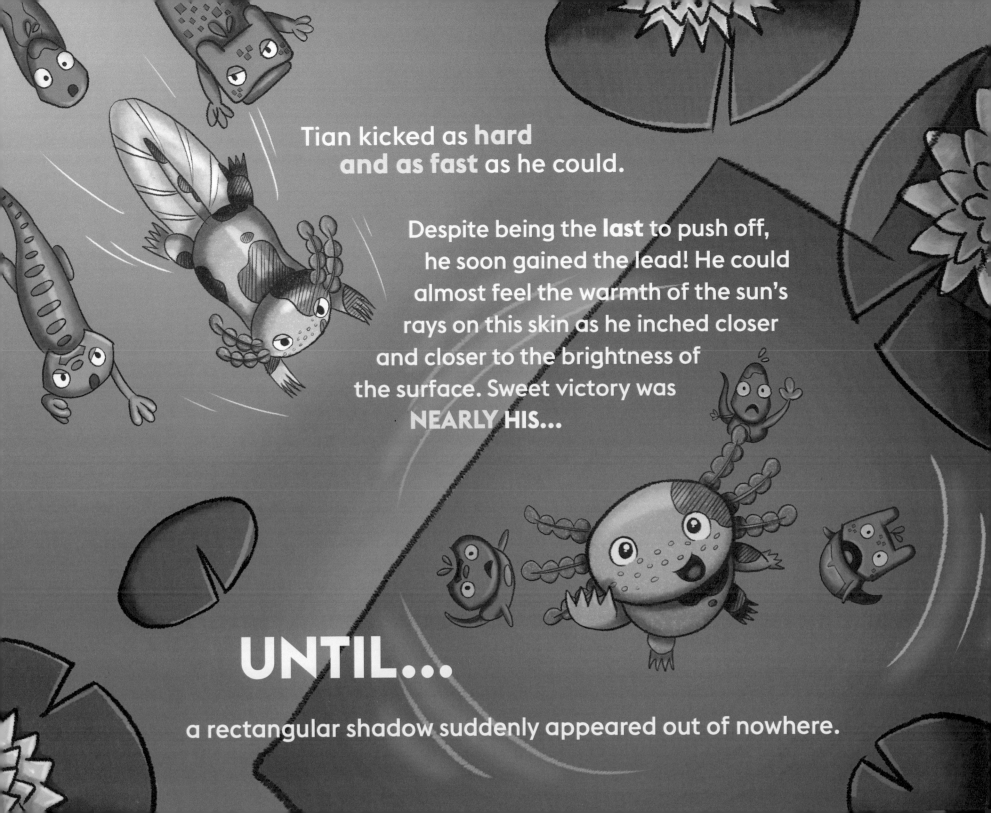

Tian kicked as **hard and as fast** as he could.

Despite being the **last** to push off, he soon gained the lead! He could almost feel the warmth of the sun's rays on this skin as he inched closer and closer to the brightness of the surface. Sweet victory was **NEARLY HIS...**

# UNTIL...

a rectangular shadow suddenly appeared out of nowhere.

Before he knew it, a canoe paddle from a passing *trajinera* sliced through the water...
(trah-hee-neh-rah)

...and sent him and the others right back
to the bottom of the lake.

**Two** hours had passed and the afternoon had turned to night.

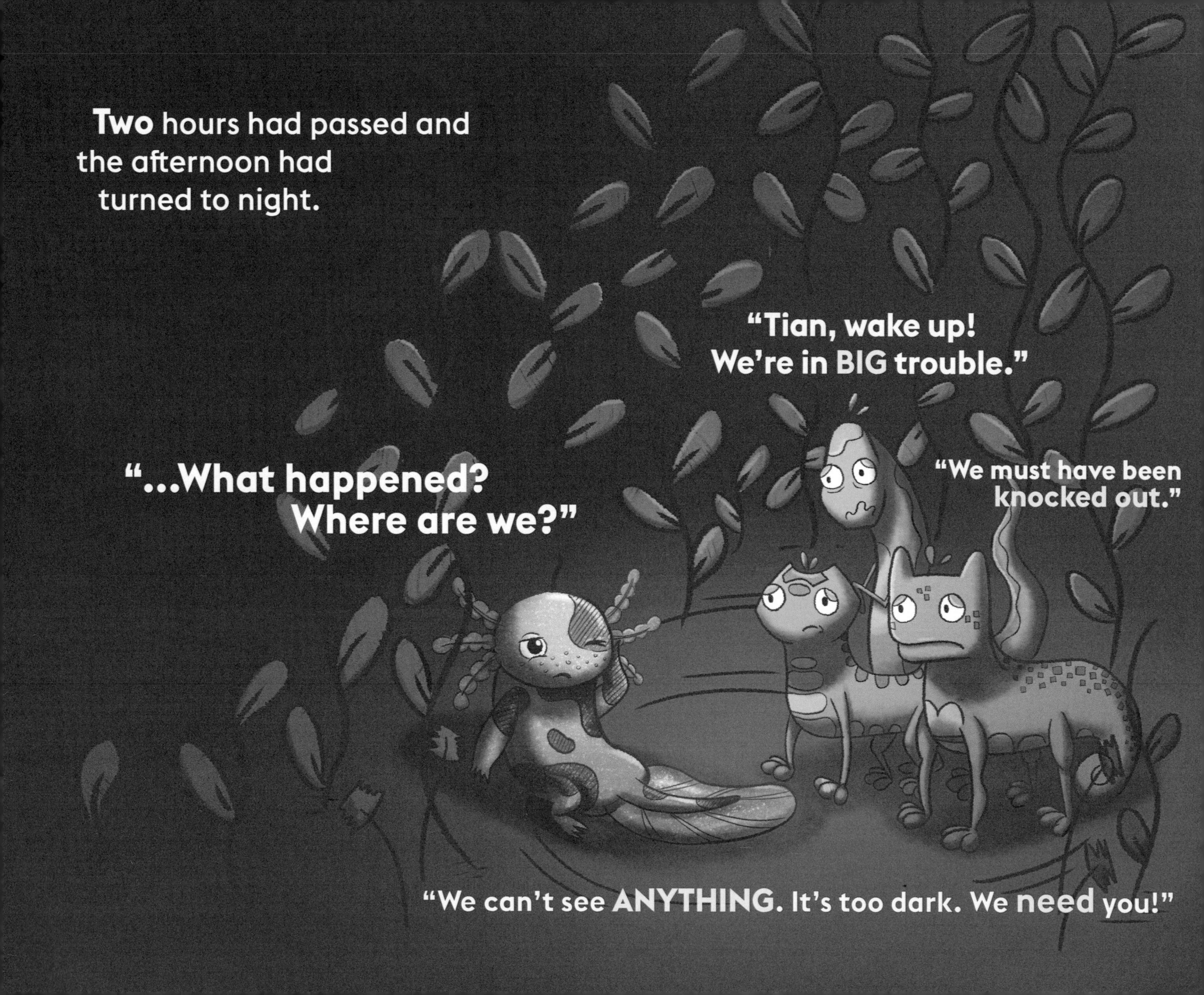

Tian finally understood that he didn't need to change who he was to love himself. He was exactly who he was meant to be and being different **WAS** his superpower. In that moment, Tian started to **GLOW AGAIN**.

With his newfound **GLOW** leading the way,
Tian and the other salamanders quickly
found their way out of the weeds
and back home to **safety.**

Legend has it that Tian's trail of light could be seen that night even by those who were near the surface of the lake.

From that day on nobody could deny Tian's **worth** or **beauty**. Not because his appearance had changed, but because his beauty ...

... GLOWED FROM **WITHIN**.

Lightning Source UK Ltd.
Milton Keynes UK
UKRC031141060223
416540UK00001B/18

* 9 7 9 8 9 8 7 0 5 6 0 0 4 *